CW00421656

CAREERING THROUGH PARENTHOOD

by Eleanor MacKenzie

(a Fullarton family)

Contents

1

INTRODUCTION

Bringing up three boys, and working full-time there's barely enough time for anything. But to preserve sanity there's always enough time to jot down the comedy moments of the day and record them for posterity – or at least long enough to embarrass those concerned.

There are no manuals for parenthood, certainly none that the baby has read beforehand. There are however great expectations about how life is going to be, forged by watching how other people parent. As if that was any guide at all.

And if a second child comes along – or indeed a third – there is the expectation that having the same parents, being brought up in the same house and subject to the same rules will mean that the child will be much the same as his older sibling. What a shock to find out that the tried and tested – or let's be honest, random - parenting techniques used on the first child are of no use at all with the second and third.

As a coping mechanism throughout the years when I was bringing up one, then two, then three boys, I made a point of scribbling down some of the highlights on the fridge as they happened, for my own records and to amuse the grandparents. A fair few made their way onto social media. Recording these incidents kept me sane, as if controlling how I wrote up the incident reminded me just for a moment that I could make sense of the randomness of the conversations I was having and help me cope with whatever the next minute was going to throw at me.

The stories recorded here are all true; although to preserve blushes most have been anonymised to disclose only the age of the child involved, rather than their position in the family. I hope you enjoy reading them as much as I have enjoyed remembering them.

EM

CHAPTER ONE: THE PRE-SCHOOL YEARS

Gretchen Rubin writes: "The years are short, but the afternoons are long."

Nowhere is this more apt when dealing with the pre-schoolers, who looking back grow up quicker than I ever thought possible. However there are times when each day, each hour, particularly of the early days of maternity leave, seems to stretch interminably between mealtimes, when you look forward to any prospect of adult company.

These were the days when Darling Husband came in with news of his workplace and inside my head I was itching for him to finish so that I could share with him the ground-breaking news that I had found a new way to walk to the supermarket which only involved negotiating one set of traffic lights. These were also the days when said Husband was able to assess within two minutes of coming through the door: "You haven't spoken to anyone today, have you?" These were the days when I positively rejoiced at the market researcher who randomly rang the doorbell and ended up inviting her in for a chat.

But the pre-school years also cover the years at nursery, the excitement of looking at frost on blades of grass, cracking the ice on puddles and watching them dress up randomly at all times of the day. And night.

From my twelve years of dealing with pre-schoolers, here are some of the notable moments.

Is there anything more exciting than being three and going to bed with your first torch?

Loving the Nursery Art Time-Lag.

Day 1: Toddler comes home in a jumper covered in orange paint.

Day 2: Toddler comes home with picture featuring yes, orange paint.

Am hoping that the two year old has proved to his satisfaction that raw eggs do not bounce.

There I stood, peeling veg. Behind me, supposedly playing with his toys, stood the toddler. And then I heard an unusual noise and spotted to my alarm a second egg being thrown to the floor.

"Here's a cake I made for you Mum at nursery. It was very good of me, wasn't it?

Can I have a bit?"

Here I am, toilet training for the third and final time. "Pants" is a fair assessment of how it's going so far...

Collecting the four year old from nursery, the conversation went thus:

"Did you know, Mum, that men can dress as ladies and ladies can dress as men?"

Instantly a letter was forming in my mind. Yes, diversity issues had to be discussed with children at some stage but really, was nursery an appropriate time and place for discussions on cross-dressing?

"Yes," he went on, "ladies can dress as men and men can dress as ladies. It's called Pantomime!!".

Mental letter scrunched up.

Shopping with the over-tidy four year old. He comes out of an in-store toilet alone with the horrifying words:

"Mum it was so weird. Some woman left her glove in the toilet. So I just flushed it."

To the woman who expected to retrieve her glove, sorry.
To the John Lewis toilet attendant/plumber, sorry.

If it's any consolation I am still blushing more than six years on.

The 5yr old opens a birthday card to find a note saying "I love you" from his nursery pal Jemima.

"Why does she love me?" he mused.

Before we could venture an answer, he said:

"It must be because I am good with buildings and inventions"

Just back from the third children's party in two days. Nobody quite does anarchy like the under 5s pumped up on sugar. Hopefully he'll sleep tonight!

And so the time came to go for a photo shoot with all three boys, then aged 2,5 and 9, taken just a week before Middle Son started school. After answering some form of questionnaire I was advised that I had "won" a photo shoot at a local photographer. Call me cynical, but this "win" seemed to entail a large expense on the resulting photos.

Each boy was to wear pastel colours and to bring along a toy of his choice. I was shown examples of this – a family photo where everyone had brought along the musical instrument that they played, a photo shoot with the family pet. "Whatever they choose to bring I'll work it in to the photos," the photographer said.

I decided to leave it up to each boy to bring what he thought he would like to bring. One son chose some technology. Another son chose a soft toy. So far, so typical.

We always suspected that the other son had a vivid imagination. What we couldn't have imagined however was that for his special toy he would choose to bring along a plastic toy credit card and a wooden spoon.

It's fair to say the photographer wasn't expecting that. Neither "toy" made the final cut in the photos.

It's 2.45am.

I am reduced to helpless laughter at the sight of the three year old announcing, "I can't get to sleep, Mum."

Although I left him in his pyjamas tucked up in bed more than seven hours ago, he is now dressed in a full Fireman Sam outfit, complete with helmet.

"Let's try losing the uniform, son and see if that makes a differ-ence."

Conversation with the 4yr old on the way to nursery:

"You go down the ramp, Mum, with the pram. I'll go down the steps, 'cos I've got my legs."

CHAPTER TWO: SCHOOL DAYS

The differences between children in the same family surface at various points, but nowhere has this manifested more clearly than in how each has navigated their school days, in both primary and secondary.

Some parents' nights have been dreaded, some welcomed. There has been an air of incredulity from staff that one son is related to the other, so different have they been in school. The parents are the same, the house is the same, the rules are the same but the children are very different.

Parents night.
Didn't see the newsbook but got a taste of it by looking at the list of words he has felt the need to ask how to spell. Predictably, "brother", "Christmas" and "holiday" but "massage"???

> ➤ Mum, there's the boy that "V"-d me today at school….
> ➤ Well just ignore him, son.
> ➤ Why would I ignore him Mum? He was in the team that I played against at football today.

➢   Ah, that kind of "V"-ing…..

Health Week in the school: turning out better than expected for our boy who never lets a piece of fruit and veg touch his lips. His teacher is giving him a personal point for every day he brings a healthy snack to school. Fortunately for him, it's the bringing and not the eating that's credited, so by leaving it uneaten in his bag, he doesn't miss out on any points. And it can be recycled for another brother, another day.

And so it was the open afternoon today at the school, complete with art exhibition and each class was allocated a different artist to use as inspiration. The 7yr olds had Matisse.

I was given the low-down on the exhibition. "Some of the pictures are really good, Mum. I actually think they are better than Matisse's."

➢   Mum, will there be homework in Heaven?
➢   Hmmm, I'm not sure….the Bible says there'll be no more pain and suffering in Heaven…..
➢   Great! That must mean no homework.

Must remember to wear specs to collect the new Primary 1 boy from school. Yesterday there was the sorry sight of a teacher doing the "I'm sure she'll be here" talk to her pupil while I stood at the back of the crowd. I hadn't recognised him in his uniform. Oops.

The 6yr old has had a spot-check and is over the chickenpox. He's heading back to school today.

"Yippee!" he said. "Finally!"

Even allowing for the age difference, proving yet again that children brought up in the same house can be so different.

Amidst the usual Monday morning debates about how ill you need to be to miss school, dinner money, the necessity of breakfast etc, I had a completely off-the-wall conversation with one of the boys about how fabulous his new socks are, how soft they are, and just the right size.

Ah the joy of some positive feedback. I was quite bowled over.

Porridge for breakfast accompanied by the refrain of "You're not ill enough to be off school."

Must be September.

Theatre traditions aside, on the day of the Primary 7 show it feels as if I am tempting fate too much to say to a performer "Break a leg".

"See in the Easter Assembly, Mum, I'm going to be a Tangerine!

No, sorry I meant Tambourine."

Yep, that's a whole lot clearer.

"Mum, come quick! There's a bird in the garden and I think it's a dodo!"

Sigh. Not for the first time, the internet research has omitted one critical point.

It's a woodpigeon.

Home today after the squelchiest school trip ever with 10 yr olds orienteering in the local country park. The washing machines will be on overdrive this weekend.

Here are my favourite quotes:

"This is brilliant; my mum doesn't let me go into the mud!"

"This is the deepest puddle ever!"

"Mrs MacKenzie, see when you were my age, which is probably 10 years ago...." (he's a charmer but needs to work on his arithmetic)

Question for the 8yr old:

"So after your school dinner, do you put the tray in a rack?

"Why would I put it there, Mum? That's a country."

"I love Fridays, Mum; they're my favourite day of the week. Want to know why? Well first of all we have a writing test...."

After 10+ years of having more than one child in the family the surprising thing is that I still expect them to be the same...... when they are self-evidently not.

CHAPTER THREE: SCOTLAND'S FOR ME

When you start Googling the lyrics of "Bonnie Wee Jeanie McColl" - that's when you know it's time to go to bed.

In London for 48 hours alone, a rare trip away from home.

Favourite moment of the day : when a car tooted and my first thought was "Ooh, maybe it's someone who knows me..."

You can take the girl out of Ayrshire, but you can't take Ayrshire out of the girl.

Hardest question of the weekend from the 5, 7 & 9 year old contingent:

"What are the Krankies? Describe them in one word, Mum"

I settled for "Scottish."

Warned the boys this morning that it was April 1st and not to be taken in by any April Fools.

"Nae danger, Mum" came the response.

We were listening to Sinatra singing "New York."

"Mum, see New York, it's always used in the films. All the super-heroes go there like Spiderman and Iron Man. Why don't they use a place in Scotland? I mean, Kilwinning's a good place...."

Visit Scotland/Visit Ayrshire, over to you. Good luck with that one.

Having a particularly Scottish moment: wearing a pinny whilst making pancakes on a girdle, while listening to Take The Floor's Scottish dance music on Radio Scotland.

It could be 1950 if it wasn't for the smartphone.

Scottish words are great:

Years ago I begin coughing uncontrollably in church one Sunday during sermon. Elderly man sitting nearby passes me a foosty mint imperial. I hesitate a minute. Guessing what I'm thinking he whispers to me:

"'S'aright, hen. Just spit oot the first sook."

Family gathering, an excuse to get out that old Glasgow joke which I don't think I'll ever tire of:

- Would you like a doughnut? Or a meringue?

- No, you're right enough, I'll take the doughnut.

Overheard in Kilmarnock this morning - truth often funnier than fiction:

"So who are you supporting in the Cup Final?"
"Ah don't know. Ah'm just gonna sit down and watch it and be neutered."

I wasn't watching the Scotland match last night but I did hear the in-house commentary on it that was being offered by one member of the family.

Amidst all that was said/shouted/screamed in a highly charged match the most memorable was "I never doubted you for a minute, Scotland!"

Not really borne out from what I heard in the previous 88 minutes, but I guess that's all part of supporting our national team.

"Look Mum, it's the Eiffel Tower. I've been up there."

"No you haven't. That was Kilwinning Abbey tower."

Kilwinning: easily mistaken for Paris.

CHAPTER FOUR: TRAVEL

Farewell today to the 7 seater car which I wondered might be too big. Instead it has been a integral part of family life for five years.

Packing in 6 footballers for a football match, 4 cricketers and their massive kitbags, multiple violas and a sax, a bike or 4, grandparents and 3 grandchildren in the same car, golfers with three sets of clubs. Arguments over Classic FM versus West FM. Hurtling down the M74 south, the A82 north, trips on Calmac ferries, getting lost in York, in Greenock, in Cumnock.

Edging oh-so-close to a Porsche in a narrow steep street at Crail Harbour with a refrigerated fish lorry coming in the opposite direction. With an incredibly nervous passenger. Happy memories.

Any day with a successful reverse park is a good day.

6yr old's version of the Green Cross Code:

"Look right, look left, look up..".
Up???
"Yes, in case there are any rockets going to land on you".

The late train home from Glasgow. All life is here.

We passed the Porsche showroom. "Have you heard of Porsches?", I asked the boys. "Sure," came the response, "That's what Aunt Lorraine has."

Eh no, that would be a Peugeot....

All ready to head back up the road after a few days at Butlins, Skegness. Noting with slight alarm (but frankly, little surprise) that one of the boys has seen fit to pack his kazoo for the car journey.

When you've picked up a son in the car from an evening activity and he starts chatting. And even though you are back home in the driveway and it's quite late and dark and there are other things to do you don't want to break the magic by getting out the car and into the house because that will stop the conversation. And you know it might be months before he starts talking like this again.

That.

An understated but momentous occasion today; youngest son was measured today and no longer needs a car seat. He was delighted and walked off looking taller than his 8 years. This brings to an end our Car Seat Years where we've gone from one car seat, to two, to three, to two then finally only one.

Rock-a-tots carrying precious, scary newborns. Rock-a-tots carrying heavy eight-month olds that nearly break your arm. Bucket seats that are impossible to keep clean because if you take them apart you will never get the straps back the right way round. Bucket seats with removable pads for toilet training. Booster seats with removable backs that were put in the loft and never traced again when we needed to put the back on again for the younger child.

There's plenty more parenting to be done in the years ahead. But today feels (in Churchill terms) to be the End of the Beginning, which began nearly seventeen years ago with the words: "Oh my goodness, you're pregnant, aren't you?"

CHAPTER FIVE: CLEANLINESS…..IS NEXT TO GODLINESS

Quote of the day: from the six year old:

"But it's Monday, Mum. I NEVER wash my hands on a Monday…"

shudder

I announce to the seven year old that I am going to run him a bath.

"Mum, see the bath, do I need to get washed in it?"

Sigh.

"I don't need to brush my hair Mum. I'm attractive already."

This boy: I gave birth to him, but there are some days when I can't believe he's my son.

It was a quiet news day so at tea I told the story about a friend's son who didn't realise that he had to use shower gel when getting washed.

There was a pause. Then a teenager pipes up: "I'm not going to lie, Mum. Sometimes I do that. I didn't think I needed to use it every time."

How did I manage to get to the stage of needing a follow up question for issues of personal hygiene:

Have you brushed your teeth...did you use toothpaste?
Have you had a shower....did you use shower gel?

"Mum, can we phone God up?"

The 4yr old saying the Lord's Prayer:

"And deliver us from The Weeble."

"Well, he's got brown hair and a silver costume."

The 6yr old describing God.

The baby must have been relieved to have his christening over with as his big brother had been going around telling everyone that there was going to be a special service for the baby on Sunday – he was going to be crucified.

Conversation with the 6yr old:

- ➢ Where do horses sleep at night?
- ➢ On a farm?
- ➢ But what's the name of the actual building?
- ➢ Don't know.
- ➢ Here's a clue: it's the place where Jesus was born...
- ➢ Bethlehem?

CHAPTER SIX: BROTHERLY LOVE

It's hard to imagine what it might have been like parenting girls as opposed to boys, but I certainly always feel an instant bond with any mother who has at least two boys. The stories I can relate to most are those generated in a house where there is more than one boy.

Two boys, two cardboard boxes, hours of fun.

October holidays.

The three boys are indulging in their current favourite pastime of wrestling. Getting more boisterous, the insults are also beginning to fly. I shout a Language Warning to them and in fairness they take action immediately. To close the door between me and them.

Not quite what I had in mind boys!

One son storms past shouting that his brother has hit him in the eye with the remote control.

The implicated brother follows him at a leisurely pace, smirking, saying that it was all an accident.

I ask the other son if he was involved in all of this. "Actually, no," he says, "it's a strange feeling. I must have matured."

Two brothers caught in the act of......playing chess. Have I wandered into a parallel universe?

"Mum, X keeps annoying me."
"Well, don't let yourself be annoyed by him."
"Why do you never say that when I'm...
[Pause as he considers he's about to incriminate himself, then resuming]
...when I'm NOT annoying him?"

No answer to that one.

One son is away on an activity holiday for a few days.

Another son has plans to take over the empty bedroom whilst he is away.

Meanwhile the other son, when he is not pretending to be a cat, thinks his big brother has gone to the moon.

Yep, situation completely normal here.

Overheard this morning. The 7yr old, addressing the 3yr old:

"So you see, that's what Vikings ate - meat. You know, like bears and things. But not pandas".

Glad we're clear on that.

One son gets up, very excited, huge grin on his face.

"Mum, guess who's going away today for a whole week?!"

It's his brother who's the one heading off.

Brotherly advice prior to the safari park trip:

"Watch you don't get eaten by the lions"

See, he does care.....

CHAPTER SEVEN:
LOVE AND MARRIAGE

Husband and wife are away for a couple of nights, attending a wedding. They book into a Travelodge and nip out to the Brewers Fayre for something to eat. A woman with a basket and shawl is going round the tables selling red roses; there may even have been a violinist too. She passes their table, but the husband calls her back, buys a rose and hands it to the wife with the immortal words:

"Do you think you could make this into a buttonhole for me to wear tomorrow?"

Tidying up the garden yesterday, cut some long stems of roses for the house, leaving them out of harm's way on the doorstep.

Cue much consternation from Darling Husband who thinks for a minute I have a secret admirer. As if.

So the question is this: at what point during the 18 years that we've been together did my Darling Husband form the view that

I would be ok about him taking some of my books to the charity shop without checking with me first?

We have now come to a fresh understanding on the issue; all is well. Look, here I am making a joke about it. Nearly.

Tutorial on strawberry picking given by the seven year old who has some experience of this, picked up from CBeebies. Strawberry picking - done. Strawberry smoothie - done. Strawberry jellies - done. Strawberry recipe hunting - done. Morrisons trip to buy extra ingredients to use up the strawberries - done.

Husband says: "I don't much care for strawberries". After 16 yrs of marriage, this comes as a surprise.

Wondering at what point my husband will explain the mysterious ladies handbag he has brought home from work. 2 and a half hours it is so far and counting.

Son develops mysterious vomiting bug the night that there is furniture to be moved. Call me a cynic but this is suspicious.

Husband and wife manage between them to move one bed, four chests of drawers, two wardrobes and a settee. Without falling out. Call me a cynic but this is miraculous.

It's mid-November. I am told I was talking in my sleep the other night at 3am. I am told that I uttered the phrase, "But it's our anniversary tomorrow!"

What I do not need to be told is that this triggered blind panic in Darling Husband, convinced it was a summer's day we got married...

I am sustained through the 1.45am deep and meaningful chat with the three year old only by the thought that it will be his dad's turn to deal with it tomorrow night.

Love is....husband agreeing to wife's request for the summer duvet and then, when the weather turns colder, sharing without comment the extra blanket he'd looked out for himself.

A wedding anniversary.

"Wow," says the wife. "22 years. So much has happened." Looking at the three boys, she says "I can think of three things straight off."

"Indeed," says the husband, "Kilmarnock have won the Scottish Cup, the League Cup and have survived without relegation in the top flight of Scottish football all that time."

Sigh.

CHAPTER EIGHT: IT SHOULDN'T HAPPEN TO A LAWYER

The contrast between life in the office and life spent with young children has been quite marked. Walking down the street with a suit and briefcase people recognise and nod hello whereas the following day when walking down the same street pushing a buggy I appear to be invisible to them.

For ten years I worked part-time where the distinction between my days in the house and my days in the office was noticeable. For one thing, I could drink a cup of coffee at work whilst it was still hot.

Here are some of the work-related memories through the years:

That moment when you come home from work and find husband and two boys singing with gusto in the kitchen: "Yo ho, yo ho a pirate's life for me!"

I should have known not to text and walk at the same time. Skinned knees and burst tights are not a good look in the office.

As a student, I considered working for the UN. Now I do work for the UN - Peacekeeping Force: Ayrshire Division. And I'm not talking about my paid employment.

The parking charges have been reintroduced at work so I have taken to parking a distance away and cycling the rest on the folding bike. No special clothes bar a waterproof and a bicycle clip, fold bike under desk, all fine. It has become part of the routine that I don't really think about it.

I must remember the next time not to pop out at lunchtime to Asda for the tea. Or if I do, to remember that it's all to fit in the bike pannier. The baguette was particularly tricky.

Next time possibly a string of onions and a beret?

Tentatively I break the news to the older brother that I am returning to work next week after maternity leave and that he will be going back to his childminder.

"Finally!" he exclaims in delight, clearly relishing the prospect of some quality childcare.

I was listening to the Balamory CD in the car for a full 10 minutes this morning before I realised that I had already dropped all the children off at nursery. Oops.

Waiting on the boiler repair man and reflecting how nice it would be to have a job where everyone is pleased to see you.

I realise I have been wandering around for goodness knows how long with only one "pane" in my glasses. It's not a good look when you're trying to be taken seriously.

Embarrassing moment of the day at work: allowing someone else to access YouTube on your phone and realising that your previous search was "Rastamouse Theme Tune."

It's a full moon tonight. I haven't seen or dealt with any behaviour either at the office or at home that could be possibly be attributed to that. Nope. No way. Absolutely not.

That moment when you're still at work and realise you should be at parents' night. Oh dear.

I was at court this morning. My phone switched off as usual. Sadly the alarm I had set to remind myself to buy milk wasn't. Alarm went off in court. It was the Wimbledon Theme tune. I am still cringing.

When you mix up the phrases: "need to be at the top of my game" and "on the ball" and you inadvertently announce to your work colleagues that you are "on the game."

Not good.

The office pedometer challenge is over. The family asked how our team had got on.

"5th!" I reported.
"What, out of 6?" they asked.
"No, out of 22!"

I should have left it there. Instead I pressed on:

"So basically, in football terms, 5th out of 22 would equate to a place in Europe"
"Only if you were in the Premiership, Mum. Not if you were in the Vauxhall Conference League"

#harsh.

A day of mixed fortunes at work:

On the one hand, I lost some inches from my hips (good)

On the other, my trousers fell down in work car park (not good)

It proved a good decision to wear the long coat.

Password paralysis: when you can't remember your password but don't want to set a new one because the new password won't be as good as the first one which was a great password, but for the fact that you can't remember it.

Nothing quite focusses the mind to hurry up in the work showers than the four words:

"Emergency Evacuation Foil Blanket"

shudder

CHAPTER NINE: ACQUIRED WISDOM

Parenthood brings its own learning across so many areas. Want to know where the nearest toilet is in any particular town: I'm your woman. How to remove an Elastoplast from a baby's hair? Oh yes, a skill I picked up along the way. Ideas to keep a toddler amused during a church service, however? Maybe you could let me know....

Mostly this wisdom has been acquired the hard way and each nugget has its own experience behind it. I share them to prevent others having to learn them the hard way.

Life Lesson No.542:

She who buys the Halloween sweets early ends up buying them twice.

Note to self: Don't use the term "bosom buddies" with the boys.

If I listen carefully I can still hear echoes of the peels of laughter.....

Remembering once again that when the washing basket is empty it means not that the washing is up-to-date, but that someone is hoarding dirty washing in their room...

3yr old to his mother:

"Are you thinking what I'm thinking?"

Based on past experience this is highly unlikely.

Note to self:

When the 8yr old is in tears crying "Mum, it really really hurts"
AND
he is clutching his chest and declaring that he is unable to walk even a few steps without extreme pain.
THEN
before you work out who will care for the others when you take him to Casualty, you might want to ask him if he was, say, running the length of the hall and launching himself onto the stage, landing on his tummy and whether that might have something to do with his pain.

Just a thought.

I'd discourage anyone who has run out of dishwasher tablets from putting a spot of washing up liquid in there instead - unless of course they are after the "bubbles creeping everywhere" look on the kitchen floor... Another cracking day of discoveries.

CHAPTER TEN: JUST A TYPICAL DAY

How can there possibly be a typical day when you are bringing up three boys? The variety of the conversation with them, the number of random questions they ask, the sheer absurdity of some situations I found myself in.

On so many occasions the only thing which kept me sane was thinking "Must write that down"…..."the grandparents will like this one"…..or "this will be an embarrassing story for them when they grow up."

 - So Mum, I was thinking about what names I would call my children when I grow up.
- Oh?
- I thought I would choose Dom for a boy.
- Really?
- Yes. It's short for Dumbledore.

Another random conversation Chez MacKenzie.

Me: Time to get up, son.

Son: The light's so bright. Is that the Angel of the Lord?

Me: Eh, no.

I am dreading the back story as to how a fully-formed birds nest (no chicks, no eggs) came to sit innocently on our garden table. The full story is not yet clear although when I raised it with the seven year old his opening remark was:

"Oops"

Do you think there might be a market for a confidential social media network for say parents, say of teenagers, to be able to ask advice/give support/ generally just wail in complete privacy away from the eyes of their offspring? Asking for a friend.

Also my friend wonders if there is anyone out there willing to share any pearls of wisdom they have gleaned on (for example) teenagers just for the purpose of encouraging others.

Thanks in advance. On behalf of my friend.

Finding it hard to take seriously any three year old who begins some of his sentences: "May I remind you....."

Not sure if I want to be told which parent he takes that from.

I have seen it all now.

It's 10.30pm, the house in silence apart from the three year old whom I discovered attempting to sneak a full litre tetra pak of orange juice out of the fridge into his bedroom.

Conversation with the 5yr old:

- Stop running over the furniture!

- But Mum, I'm good at it!

- That's not really the point.

Unexpected comedy moment of the morning:

Two brothers carrying-on in the kitchen. Plate of Rice Krispies spills all over the floor. (I am not laughing at this point.)

In the midst of sweeping up the mess, one brother mounts the brush to give a quick impression of Quidditch.

I have had a top class day, the highlight of which was a girlie lunch with my four year old niece.

Any concerns that we might run out of things to talk about were soon allayed once she got going!

Favourite moment of the week already:

The six year old standing in front of the mirror idly brushing his hair while singing under his breath "You Are My Sunshine"

Another cracker of an afternoon. I come home early from work to pick up the boys. We are sitting having a snack when a robin hops into the kitchen and starts flying around.

I jumped out my skin when I saw it and it took some time before I could persuade it back into the great outdoors. Goodness knows how long it was in the house.

There was a cagey response from the boys when I asked if they knew anything about it.

Mother, father and a son are in the kitchen washing up.

"I didn't realise it was free to call Childline," says the son.

There is a pause. Parents exchange glances before asking him if there is anything he feels the need to talk about with Childline.

"I didn't say I wanted to call them, I was just saying I didn't know it was free."

We do however consider ourselves on notice.

Summer life chez MacKenzie.

- Mum, if you're needing anything soft I've got some hay in my pocket.

- That looks like grass cuttings to me. Did you have plans for them?

- I thought I might make a bird's nest or something.

- Hmm. Maybe just put them in the bin?

- Ok

Cottage Hospital Week 4 update:

With Darling Husband now in the fourth week of complete bed rest under doctor's orders, Son#3 now has chickenpox. For the second time. "At least I can still talk, Mum" was his comment. Indeed.

Whilst there is another patient to look after, that's one less set of homework and after-school taxi driver commitments. Every cloud...

I feel a bit like Madame Cholet from Wimbledon Common ie responsible for feeding everyone, getting into the odd tizzy and generally keeping all those naughty young Wombles in check. Both patients are recovering steadily but impatiently.

7yr old to the 3yr old on the nature of comedy:

"Mum doesn't find you funny because you don't have the pair of pants on your head."

The 4yr old is choosing a new word or phrase every day to teach the baby. Rather than any state of the art early intervention literacy programme, this is an attempt to prevent the baby shouting "Poo!" at every opportunity.

It is working to a point, although some of the phrases chosen have been quite surreal.

Today "penguin". Yesterday "cheese and chutney sandwiches."

As Robert Burns nearly said: " The best-laid schemes of mice and mums are often jiggered by a trip to A&E"

I thought I'd had a bad day until I went to collect the three year old from nursery and discovered that he had been stung by a wasp.

On the nose.

It's only Thursday and so far this week the family have had an emergency GP appointment, a routine hospital appointment, an unexpected operation, a referral for an eye operation and two emergency Collect Your Child From School calls. Which I think is a record even for us.

If anyone is having a similar week, can I suggest you join me (in a virtual sense), for a large gin and a rousing rendition of "I'm still standing" at 9pm on Friday. Although perhaps that is tempting fate.

One boy back to school after three days off last week, one boy sick yesterday and off school today, one boy sent home today from school.

One thing I know for sure: the careers adviser was right not to suggest nursing as an option for me.

When the nine year old says "'Nothing to worry about Mum, nothing to worry about. Everything is under control."

It's time to worry.

CHAPTER ELEVEN: TOOTHBRUSHING AND THE TRIALS OF THE TOOTH FAIRY

What is it about the Tooth Fairy? Please tell me that other parents are as remiss about this as I am. Our Tooth Fairy rarely comes on the relevant night, frequently forgets, and throughout all dealings I have no idea whether I have shared the secret with the Tooth Fairy with any or all of the children. Where money is still being received however, it's fair to say their ears may be closed to hearing the reality.

The seven year old has announced his tooth has finally come out.

This will of course involve money, but unfortunately I can't remember if he is still at the tooth fairy stage. Better play it safe and go through the rigmarole - tomorrow night.

Son#3 finally loses a first tooth. The Tooth Fairy has now been in service for nine years and still she's in danger of forgetting.

Mother to son:

- Have you done your teeth?
- Yes.
- Tonight?

(Pause. Son slinks off stage left.)

Bother bother bother. The Tooth Fairy has once again forgotten. I think she possibly got caught up watching the Champions League final.

All the 6yr old wants for Christmas is one of his front teeth.

"Mum, months and months went by, but now it's happened" said the 8yr old in a dramatic fashion.

His wobbly tooth has finally fallen out.

Toothbrushing Episode 543

- Have you done your teeth?
- Yes
- Tonight?
- Yes.
- So that means you'll be smelling sweetly of toothpaste?
- Well no, actually. I just said yes before to put you off. Does this mean I have to brush my teeth every night?

Sigh.

CHAPTER TWELVE: BOOKS, BOOKS AND BOOKS – AND THE GOOD BOOK

The joy of a good book. The joy of choosing a good book. The joy of sitting down in peace and quiet to enjoy a good book. Throughout the early years there was a definite downturn in personal bookreading.

It was however a delight to share books with the children and watch them - well, some of them, some of the time - learning to love books too. I could have done with slightly less Thomas the Tank Engine however.

After the best part of two years, plenty of laughs, corny accents and quite a few tears I have now finished reading the Harry Potter series to the eleven year old. I feel a bit bereft now it's over! If only we had another book in the house to read......(ahem)

Fresh from BB Bible knowledge night, I asked the boys in the car for names of people who had lived for a long time ie around 200 years.

Answers I was expecting: Adam, Noah, Methuselah.

Answers I was not expecting (but received): Papa Smurf and Yoda.

Keep revising boys!

Caught the 10 year old reading tonight. Without it being suggested to him. Life is good!

Just went through to one of the boy's rooms. He was sitting reading.

- What are you reading son?

- I'm just reading this section of the book called "Latin phrases every schoolboy should know"

Three boys: same parents, same house, same rules. Completely different.

"Our class is doing the Easter Assembly Mum! We've to find out all about Good Sunday. And Palm Friday."

(Nice to see that he's been paying attention in Sunday School for the past 9 years.)

Was ushered out a son's bedroom as he wanted to read. Alone. Get into those books, boys!

"Well, he's got brown hair and a silver costume...". The 6yr old on the subject of God.

Any day in which I have a random discussion with the eight year old and have cause to utter the line:

"No, I don't think there were any unicorns in the Bible" has to qualify as a good day.

Another classic conversation with the 5yr old:

- Can you tell me what's going on here?

- Well I couldn't find a bookmark so I just used my pants.

Clean, I should say, but still....

CHAPTER THIRTEEN: HOUSE AND GARDEN

It's not every day you go to shout the children in for tea and discover they are all working together to dig a secret tunnel passageway in the garden. The hole is in the middle of a flowerbed, around a foot and a half in diameter and a couple of feet deep. I catch them mid-dig. The ten year old is holding a shovel, the six year old a junior size spade and the two year old a trowel.

Feeling uncharacteristically chilled, instead of ranting immediately at them, I ask a few questions. They are unsettled by this approach.

- Wow, boys, this looks interesting.
- We're digging a secret passageway!
- I see. Where to?
- See that yellow bush at the far end of the garden – that's where it's going to finish.
- Ah, so you're going to dig under the entire vegetable patch?
- Yes.
- That sounds great - let me know how you get on!

Completely floored by the lack of a row, the six year old blurts out with all the information I need to know.

- We thought you'd go mental Mum! That's why Dad said not to tell you.

Thank you Universe.

It wisnae me who used the wrapping paper last.

- "Mum, I've just been thinking"

- Hmm? (Deep intake of breath)

- "This would be a great house if there was a zombie apocalypse."

Just to let you know: you're all welcome.

Eight year old found hoovering his bedroom without being asked. My first thought: "What evidence is he trying to hide?"

The 7yr old in frustration:

"But my room's too tidy, Mum. I can't find a thing!"

Despairing yet again at seven year old. Spotted him playing Rock Paper Scissors with his reflection in his bedroom. He seems surprised it's a dead heat each time.

Has finally obtained an explanation from the twelve year old son for the shallow dishes of water and porage oats sitting neatly on a pillowcase in his wardrobe.

Son: "Well, I was going to catch a bird and keep it in there".
Mother: *speechless*

Mother to a son:

I found your jumper - it was in your bedroom. Was it:
(a) hanging in your wardrobe?
(b) folded neatly in a drawer?
(c) rolled up in a ball on your chair?

Son: I think I'm going to strike out (a) and (b) as options...

I knew the 6yr old's room was a mess.

What I didn't expect to find there was the handle from the Sunday School cupboard.

Was tidying the garden at the weekend to find that boys have taken the hole/start of a secret passageway they dug last summer to a new level by lining it with copious black bags filling it on the sly with the hose and calling it a pond. As if there isn't enough Wild Life in the garden.

Is hoping that the "Bunnies For Sale" sign in a house along the road from us is taken down soon before it is noticed by the junior members of the family.

One of the stick insect eggs appears to have hatched. Possibly yesterday or the day before, or last week; the diligent daily checking has dwindled recently.

Don't know much about them yet but guessing they don't usually lie on their backs with legs in the air. RIP wee man, it's probably for the best.

It's science fortnight in the school, coupled with a Natural Disasters topic. The washing machine is on its final spin and the sink is full of washing-up water.

"Look Mum, the water is vibrating. That's either from the washing machine or we are having an earthquake."

Good to keep an open mind.

When you have a Saturday list of jobs to do in a tight time frame. And you start hoovering. And a teenage son shouts something at you from outside the room. And you shout back that he'll need to come in to the room if he's got something to say. And you continue hoovering.

And he shouts even louder from outside the room. And you shout back yet louder. And again he shouts louder. And in complete exasperation you switch off the hoover, about to let rip and turn round to find...

....it's not your teenage son but your cycling minister, drenched in sweat who has popped in for a glass of water.

#Savedbythehoover
#Savedbygrace

Things I Should Have Hidden Better:

"Mum! You've got a glue gun!"

Had an afternoon session baking with two of the children. Nowadays this consists of me doing the baking and them posing about pretending to be Mel and Sue from The Great British Bake Off.

My favourite type of misdialled number.

- Hello, is that "Natural Beauty"?

So tempted to reply:

- Why of course!

Open freezer.
Grab nearest container of soup.
Heart sinks.
"Brussel Sprout Soup 3/1/17."

That's what we call a Recipe Regret.

November '11: make biscuits. Son turns nose up at them.

December '11; make same biscuits for same son, with addition of 3 chocolate chips per biscuit.

Son declares that they are the best biscuits ever.

Contemplating the newly-baked pancakes with the six year old:

- That one didn't really turn out, did it?

- No, it didn't Mum. (Pause) I think you should have it.

I announced the pudding: Peach upside-down cake. And back came the response: "Did you mean it Mum?"

Aged 12, one son knows exactly how his mother's homebaking works.

A maths question for the 4yr old:

"How many eggs are left in the eggbox now that we've used 2?"
"Six."
"Six??"
"Yes. But two are invisible."

I made pancakes for the boys this afternoon. "They're ok, Mum!" they said excitedly.

Shame about the surprised tone in their voices....

➢ Who made the chocolate apples?
➢ Aunt Sandra.
➢ The apple part too?
➢ No, that was God.
➢ So Aunt Sandra made the chocolate apples, helped by God.

Yep, that pretty much covers it.

CHAPTER FOURTEEN:
FILM AND TV

Nothing quite characterises the childhood years more than the TV and films watched, as well as those missed. A new blockbuster movie at the cinema? Sorry, not seen it, but I have seen Piglet's Big Movie. And Paddington.

A new must-see box set that everyone's talking about at work? No idea, nor do I know the main actors in it. But I could give you a run down of the differences between the iterations of Fireman Sam over the years, as well as tell you who lives in what coloured house in Balamory.

Star Wars fan branching out to watch different films:

- I did not realise Hans Solo was in so many movies!

#HarrisonFord

Random conversation at work about the Lego Movie:

- So did it have an inherent Legoness about it?

- That depends on how you define Legoness...

From the A Bit Slow on the Uptake Team:

"Oh I see now. He's called Ben 10 because his name's Ben and he has 10 alieny things he can do"

Slightly troubled by the effect on our collective mental health - and that of our children - of a 24 hr news service. A Pathé news bulletin before a cinema matinee announcing "Meanwhile in America...." seems preferable.

What is it about the Krankies? Both now in their late 60s, career in showbusiness over 30 years, still able to entertain in a very demanding market. The boys saw them in Panto the other day and came back raving about them.

I say: "The Krankies are a bit funny....."

The 7 year old says: "They're not funny, Mum, they're hilarious!!"

Big debate in the car at the weekend over which emergency services would be involved if a cat fell off a cliff. I'm an animal lover but am not sure that it's a job for the coastguard, fire service, RNLI and search and rescue helicopter. Fireman Sam has a lot to answer for in raising expectations.

Family dvd night. We were watching a Harry Potter film.

"So," I asked, "if you could turn yourself into any animal, which one would it be?"

"A black-handed spider monkey, Mum," he said straightaway, "because then I could dangle by my tail."

Not the answer I was expecting. He seems to have given some thought to it beforehand

Waking up in the armchair next to a cold cup of peppermint tea with an unfamiliar programme blaring having fallen once again for the ruse that I can hear the news so much more clearly if I just close my eyes for a moment ......

The two year old, showing his twin influences of the Balamory policeman and the Old Testament: "Stop in the Name of the Lord!"

I've just been told in a frank exchange with my six yr old that my feet are "just like Shrek's".   I haven't seen the film for a while, but am guessing this isn't a compliment...

Future career plans after seeing Sister Act:

"Can we [me and my brothers] be nuns when we grow up?"

I appear to be the only person in Glasgow who is neither going to, or wishing she was going to see Take That at Hampden.

As the punter in Gordon Street said, shaking his head:

"Too many wummin, hen, too many wummin".

On-the-job English lesson, first thing in the morning:

- Mum, would you go on the Great British Bake-Off?

- Yes, absolutely. Because there are times when I think I don't have enough to fill my days.

(Pause)

- Was that sarcasm, Mum?

Spot on son. Spot on.

Overheard conversation:

"Yeah, my dad used to watch Dr Who in the 1900s*."

*This is how a 9yr old refers to the years before 2000.

CHAPTER FIFTEEN: AGEING

Giving birth to the next generation inevitably brings into focus aspects of ageing and time passing by very quickly. Add to that the comments of that younger generation, blunt to the point of comical and hampered by poor arithmetic. You need to have a thick skin to be a parent!

Last weekend: kindnesses galore for Mother's Day.

This weekend: the brothers jockey for position.

"See when you and dad die, who's going to live in the house?"

Suddenly I'm not feeling as hale and hearty as I was.

"Mum, did you have electricity when you were at school?"

Who said children keep you young?

Ageing moment of the week: having to explain to a work colleague who Claire Grogan is. Going through the whole Gregory's Girl / Altered Images conversation took the edge of my astonishment as to what age she has reached. How did that ever happen?

I note that over the past few weeks I have forgotten to take the daily cup of green tea I read was good for preventing dementia.

I think this could be a case of closing the stable door after the horse has bolted.

It's amazing, the restorative power of a good night's sleep. Another thing that my parents and grandparents were right about. ("Will you get to bed, lassie!")

"Mum, our teacher was telling us a story today. About 2005, when she was a teenager...."

I didn't hear anything after that.

Disco nap: I suspect you and I are going to become good friends. If I ever get into the habit of going out on a Saturday night, that is...

"See Oreos, Mum? Were they around when Dad was a boy?

'Cos they're in black and white."

With Princes William and Harry now both married, I think it's quite ageing to hear of an engagement and wedding when you remember their parents announcing their engagement.

A dramatic afternoon:

Feeling young at the matinee in the Kings Theatre Glasgow today (hardly anyone under 60).

Feeling slightly older when realising that sitting in the seventh row of the stalls is not close enough for me to see properly without my glasses.

Feeling very old when asked by the lady behind whether I was the grandmother of my six year old.

How I laughed. Not.

Over the past couple of days I've been trying to sort out my pension. Let's just say there were no laughs in that.

Other than 1894 being a possible date of birth in the State Pension Age calculator on gov.uk. You know, just in case there were any 122 year olds hoping they could retire soon.

I know, still not funny. This is the future.

Few things mark the passage of time more cruelly than the com-pare-and-contrast-the-photo exercise between the existing pass-port and the renewal application.

Realising that I am now a nodding acquaintance of someone I don't really know, but see around regularly and say hello to them each time because I repeatedly mistake them for someone else.

I told one of the boys my primary school headmistress had died. She was 94. "Was she still working?" he asked.

CHAPTER SIXTEEN: SHOPPING

Shopping as a parent is classified in two ways: the shopping you do alone and that which you do with a child/ several children in tow. Both are best done at speed.

Shopping alone is done at breakneck pace to maximise the time whilst the children are at school/nursery. When at work coming home from a course I also perfected a quick recce around the shops on the station concourse to see if I could use the spare minutes to buy any forthcoming birthday cards or presents.

Shopping with children I found was best limited as much as possible and this is where online shopping deliveries come into their own. I still shudder at the memory of the bottle of red wine which smashed on the floor beyond the checkouts when an angry six year old wished to convey just how annoyed he was at being asked to help by carrying a shopping bag out to the car.

As ever of course, the conversations thrown up by the children whilst shopping are in a class of their own........

Standing with the 6 yr old in Marks and Spencer on Saturday, I asked him what he was thinking. This is a dangerous question, I should know by now.

"I'm just wondering how you know you can trust the people who work in shops, Mum?"

Counter-terrorism officer in the making? Possibly, but I just wished he hadn't raised it in front of the mild-mannered, grey-haired shop assistant…

Colleagues were a touch concerned when my opening question to them of the morning was:

"At what time do Asda start selling alcohol?"

Answer: 10am: not early enough…..

Save yourself money on Black Friday weekend. Leave your hand-bag in the car. (D'oh!)

LOST: One husband. Last seen heading for Asda. Two hours ago.

This weather's terrible. Went into Next at lunchtime to shelter from the rain. Bought two lamps.

Shopping according to musical tempo:

At 2 o'clock: Prestissimo.

At 6 o'clock: Adagio rallentando.

At the self service check-outs:

Can we have a bit less "Unexpected item in the bagging area" and a bit more "You've left your card in the machine, ya numpty."

Thanks to Tesco staff for reuniting card with owner.

Today we won a pound of mince from Lidl on a scratchcard. This is a set of words I never expected to see in a sentence together.

Can I just explain that there was context to the shop refusing to sell me alcohol with my newspaper at 9am this morning. I was multi-tasking and thought I'd pick up a special offer on a bottle of red.

#peskylicensinglaws

Darling Husband has clearly been brainwashing the children.

On a visit to a shoe shop the other day the two year old was heard shouting from his buggy:

"You not need shoes, Mum!" and "They not fit you, let's go home!"

Holiday shopping for husband.

TK Maxx sells menswear, not just shoes and handbags. Who knew?!

Shopping with the 5 year old yesterday.

 - "That is the biggest pea I have ever seen in my life, Mum!"

[Pause]

- "Actually, we call that a watermelon son.

CHAPTER SEVENTEEN: POLITICS

General Elections, Scottish independence, American elections, to say nothing of Brexit have all featured in discussions at the tea-table. The depth of feeling on each has taken us slightly by surprise.

Previously unheard argument around Scottish independence:

- Why, what's the matter with England?

- It's not a good place. They don't have potato scones.

Teatime discussion on Scottish independence with the primary schoolers. One says: But it might lead to fighting with the English....

 At which the other gives a "Yes!" and declares himself in favour.

Modern studies for 8yr olds:

- Where does the Prime Minister live?
- Oh wait, I know this one! Is it Quality Street?

Sigh.

One son on the subject of Jeremy Corbyn:

"Who is that guy Mum? He looks like the old version of Obi Wan Kenobi."

Who lives at 10 Downing Street?
That's easy Mum. Mother Teresa.

Teresa May, Mother Teresa....Close, but no cigar.

The 10yr old on the subject of the 2010 General Eleaction:

"I want David Cameron to win - I don't like Gordon Brown or Nick Clogs."

It's news to us that his True Blue tendencies extend beyond supporting the local football team.

CHAPTER EIGHTEEN: CLOTHING

Ever since the first milk stain from the newborn was deposited on my shoulder, clothing has never quite been the same again. The children can have very firm ideas on what they should wear, and when. And God forbid that the washing machine should ever stop working....

Also, as soon as the children can speak, comments on your clothing are made freely which is enough to dent any mother's shoogly confidence in her appearance.

Day 3 without a washing machine reveals different priorities between mother and the 4-year-old. He spills tomato soup down his football top at lunch.

NO! I cry.

Don't worry Mum, I've got another football top!

Feeling pleased with self after running 20mins non-stop in gym, caught sight of reflection in car window and spotted previously unnoticed seam in top. Was on inside out.

#gymsuccess.
#clothingfail.

Quote of the day, having picked him up from school:

"Mum, NEVER wear that hat again"

Little does he know I have a few others which I know he's going to love too.

So I said to my sister (a nurse who has spent all her working life in theatre greens): "That's great news about the new job - but do you have to wear clothes?".

To which she replied: "What kind of job do you think this is?!"

"Please Mum, can I wear a scarf? Please!"

"Ok"

"I can't believe it, I'm wearing a scarf! I'm so excited"

Oh to recapture the days of Scarf Excitement.

"Mum, you are rocking those shades by the way!"

Offspring's approval: rarely given, gratefully received.

"You're looking quite Halloween-ish today, Mum!"

Black with a flash of orange: a hard look to pull off.

The sun is shining. The 4yr old and I go out to paint the fence. I ask him to put on his old trousers first and he goes to change.

A few minutes later, wailing starts. He is having difficulty putting on his old trousers. I suggest it might be easier if he takes off his novelty fire engine slippers first.

Pause. Wailing resumes. He is still having difficulty.

I suggest that it would be easier if he takes off his nursery trousers first before putting on the painting trousers. Double trousers is not a good look.

I help him take off the old trousers, and the nursery trousers underneath them. However, underneath the nursery trousers are the muddy jeans he had been wearing before nursery. I suggest he takes them off and puts them in the washing basket.

He pauses and looks embarrassed. I ask why.

It seems that he has failed to wear any pants to nursery that morning.

Tally for the day:

Trousers attempted: 3
Trousers achieved: 2
Pants worn: 0

"Do you like my new hat, son?"

"Oh yes Mum, it's like a cake!"

Hmmm.

The 5yr old has his philosophy on life sorted out.

"One thing, Mum. I need my Spiderman pants. Or my Batman pants. They make me a superhero. That's the secret of pants."

CHAPTER NINETEEN: TECHNOLOGY

Over the seventeen years when I was dealing with an under 10 in the family, there were huge strides with technology. When the oldest was born, I didn't even have a mobile phone, but by the time the youngest was born, social media was an established fact of life to be negotiated.

And the parenting issues thrown up by technology: numerous.

Mothers with modern technology startle sons.

On the one hand they can give an unexpected report on the Killie u20s game from Twitter, much to the son's delight.

On the other hand the school can contact them by text to advise that the French homework has not been handed in, much to the son's disgust.

Here I am, destined to walk forever on the prom at Largs having failed to specify exactly where "on the front" she would meet her husband & children. At least it's a glorious day! Now if only someone would invent a phone you could carry with you... and a means of remembering to take it with you.....

Why is predictive text not yet clever enough to learn from its mistakes?

My fat fingers have often typed "hete" instead of "here" but not once have I wanted to say in a text to a fellow mum:

"In case you are looking for him, X is heterosexual and he can stay for his tea if that's ok with you"

Am adjusting to my first Smartphone. I however just caught myself trying to "left click" a link...by hitting it with a different finger. Oops.

Well done to the local boiler repair company who came out this evening to fix our new boiler. At one point this afternoon, we had no hot water, no heating and the sockets were repeatedly fusing in the kitchen meaning no fridge/cooker/microwave/kettle.

I still don't know what caused the electrical problem but I switched all items off and it seems to have righted itself. Unperturbed by the lack of heating/ kitchen facilities the younger two were outraged, saying:

"What do you mean we can't use the Xbox?"

CHAPTER TWENTY: HOLIDAYS

The theory is good: what could be more relaxing than a break away with the family?

Reality: what could be more stressful than rushing to complete all work before a break, packing up everything in the house into the car for fear of leaving behind some crucial piece of equipment which will make the break away unmanageable, living in an unfamiliar setting with over-excited children for the next week or so, before returning home to a mountain of washing? Relaxing? Oh please.

In the early days we coped with holidays by mentally drawing a four-hour-drive circle around the house and choosing a destination somewhere inside of that. As they grew older, we felt we could throw in a ferry trip to that to extend the options. It was years before we ever risked a plane. And yet wherever we went, somehow amidst the stress and the tiredness a sliver of a happy memory can creep through. And it makes it all worth it.

Noting with alarm that the 6yr old felt it necessary to pack a snorkel and flippers for a two night break up north and wondering what he's got planned: diving for Nessie?

Saturday: got up at 5am (all 6 of us - we have a bonus teenager aka honorary family member) checked out of the youth hostel, on to ferry, 4 hour journey, tracked down house, stocked up with food, unpacked the car, made up the beds etc etc.

Amidst all this, the sole conversation topic for the under 16s is the wifi in the house:

- Has anyone got the wifi working yet?
- Mum, what's the wifi password?
- I can't get this wifi working, Mum.
- I've tried every number on this box but I still can't find the password.

Sigh.

Language differences between Scotland and England:

"See in Butlins, Mum, I learned a new game called Tag.

Basically it's just like Tig.

Heard on Holiday. This could be a rich seam of material. "I can't wait to see the fairies again!". Wow, we knew the three year old had a rich imagination. Turns out we misheard. He meant the Calmac Ferries.

3 days holiday, 3 hyper sons.

1 slightly harassed mother, 2 lasagnes made for husband at home, 250 mile round trip, 2 nights in a Travelodge booked last minute in Dundee - what can possibly go wrong? Hmm, let me count the ways......

Have just suggested to the 7yr old that really he doesn't need to take Tippex with him on holiday.

Just found a tuning fork in the 9yr old's holiday packing. Well you never know when you're going to be asked for a concert A.

I note with much relief that "Oban's record breaking Strip, tonight at 6.30pm. Come and join us!" turns out to be an attempt to stage the biggest Strip the Willow. Phew.

Heard on holiday, the 7yr old to the 11yr old:

> ➤ Can I sleep in your room tonight?
> ➤ Ok. But don't bring your night-vision goggles this time.

Am now in sole charge of three children with at least two ferries to negotiate, a World Cup final and a 6.15am start. Darling Husband: we miss you already!!

Putting on the bike rack:

"Ok Mum," said the 11 yr old. "if the Youtube video showing us how to put on the bike rack on the car is only 2 minutes long, it'll only take us 5 mins, right?"

I wish.

"But Mum, I absolutely hate beaches! I really do. I'd rather have broccoli than go to a beach."

This is good news. We'll shortly be upping the broccoli intake.

Realising that my Good Hair/Good Face Day is not coming and I will just need to get the passport photo taken regardless.

I had been in for a swim.

"Mum, you look like that person from Grease!"

For a nanosecond I think he means Olivia Newton John and my heart melts.

Turns out my hair is slicked back and he meant John Travolta.

Sigh.

Back to work today after a family holiday.

Take a busy family of five which for fifty weeks of the year does umpteen different activities in umpteen different directions, often at the same time. Throw them together for two weeks 24/7, take away the wifi, take away one of their checked-in bags, ramp up the temperature to double what they're used to, add in language difficulties and car hire challenges and what do you get?

Hey, we survived! Sometimes we even laughed! We might even have managed a minute or two of relaxation.

Thankful to the family for
(a) teaching me new card games - Uppy Doonies anyone?
(b) sharing with me more information about Dr Who and Super-

heroes than I will ever need to know and
(c) indulging me in fulfilling a long-held dream to go to see the open-air opera at Verona and not complaining (much) when Aida ran to 4hrs.

[At the end of Act One] "You are kidding me Mum, there's more?"

On the first day of the holiday, the world today seems divided into those people who like to talk in the morning and those who would rather not.

Grateful that the two people in the family who like to talk in the morning can do so to each other and leave the rest of us alone.

#Coffee
#CoffeeNotConversation
#MoreCoffee

"Mum, can you go on one side of the see-saw and me and my brother go on the other to even it out?"

Sigh.

The 5yr old on a trip to Edinburgh Zoo.

"I can't wait to see the mammoths Mum!"

"Hmmm, there's been a bit of bad news on the mammoth front recently. They're extinct."

"Mum, can we go to London? I want to see Lady Pop-in. And also go up a chimney."

The 3yr old, having watched Mary Poppins.

CHAPTER TWENTY-ONE: MUSICAL MEMORIES

Music forms a big part of our household including music at school and nursery, taking part in choirs and shows or practising instruments. It has featured to varying degrees in each of the boys' lives whether that be singing on a stage or on the terraces of the local football park.

Being a parent brings a whole new perspective on music. Growing up, the recorder seemed a fine instrument; its tone only began to grate when I heard it as a frazzled parent played by a very keen 7yr old.

Here are some of the favourite musical memories:

"Great news Mum, I've found my mouth organ.

Sometimes it's extra-good to be heading out to work in the morning.

Words to gladden any mother's heart:

"Just to say that the children who have been working on the tin whistle can take them home to keep."

Lovely. Smashing. Thanks.

The 5yr old has been packing for our caravan holiday. Mercifully, after some debate, he decides to leave his bongo drums at home.

A Beatles song came on the radio. I began to outline who the Beatles were.

"We were learning a Beatles song at school, Mum," said the 6yr old. I was impressed.

It turned out to be: "The ants were marching two by two".

More Beetles than Beatles it seems.

"This is boss!
The 5yr old's worrying appraisal on Agadoo.

Some months ago:
I hide my flute in a safe place to prevent the children playing with

it.

This weekend:
I hunt high and low for the flute for half an hour. Eventually I call in the children to help out. They track it down in ten seconds.

And lo, it came to pass that the 9yr old spent his Christmas money not on the computer game he had been eyeing up, but on a ukulele. Upon which he is now playing "Polly Wolly Doodle". All the day.

- Son, have you practised for orchestra?
- Well, yes.
- All of it?
- Well actually just 4 bars.
- Which 4 bars?
- The rests.

The day a son comes from school with a chanter, keen to learn the bagpipes.

Please, no.

And so it came to pass that an alto saxophone came to live in the house.

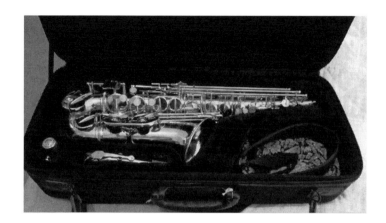

Apologies to those within earshot of our house and the local shop for the piercing "music" heard yesterday.

It turns out that the 8yr old saw fit to take his recorder with him to play as he walked to the shop to pick up the newspaper.

I have now made it clear to him that his recorder playing should be restricted to the house. And hopefully soon he'll learn a fourth note.

CHAPTER TWENTY-TWO: THINKING THE UNTHINKABLE

Here we reflect on those phrases which prior to being a parent you never thought anyone in the world would have reason to utter.

"Just to be clear, you are not taking the whoopee cushion to church"

"Now boys, I don't think you should play Hide The Toothbrush any more."

One brother is frantically searching around complaining that it's too hard; whilst the other looks casually over towards him with the words "You're getting warmer....."

- Mum, I can write a horror story in only five words.
- Really?

"Once there was no wi-fi."

"Mum, will I be able to whistle under water?"

"Just to be clear, you are not taking your plastic grenade to church.

Especially not on Remembrance Sunday."

"Gran, are fish waterproof?"

"For the last time, will you take that carrot out the washing machine please?"

CHAPTER TWENTY-THREE: HOBBIES FOR PARENTS

One of these days, I might have some spare time to spend on one of my own activities. Until then, it's snatched memories of things I used to do. We haven't moved house, but it feels as if we lived in a foreign country before the children came long.

Optimism: realising you have already bought wool for the second pair of socks you will knit. Right after you finish the first pair which stand at four rows knitted of the first sock and were last touched before the youngest child was born.

Another Monday night, another bar. But it's toasty warm with the open fire and at least I can get on with my paperwork while waiting to pick up boys.

(Picking up boys: this could have been expressed better. It's a lot less exciting than it sounds.)

The nights are fair drawing in. Time to think about picking up some sewing. It's like a trip down Memory Lane. Look: there's the cushion I was sewing for my mum and dad's silver wedding. They have now been married for more than double that time. Oh well....

3yr old to mother on seeing her playing the piano:

"Wow, when did you learn to do that?"

Ah, memories of Life Before Children.

"Wow, that's amazing Mum, I've never seen you exercising before!"

I'm still not sure how I feel about running or whether I could get serious about it, but I am serious about avoiding an injury, hence this morning's visit to a running shop to be fitted for trainers and where I ran on the treadmill to the obvious and frank astonishment of the 5yr old.

This week's gym challenge is a 2K row followed by 5K on the bike then treadmill for 3K. Not quite sure I quite recognise myself in all this but the message for you folks is "It's not too late to change."

CHAPTER TWENTY-FOUR: EXTRA-CURRICULAR ACTIVITIES

And whilst parents have only distant memories of their own hobbies, our diaries are filled to the brim with different activities for the children. Beyond that, the children themselves find more than enough adventures with which to fill their days at home.

❖ ❖ ❖

Mother to son:

Exactly what part of "Put the Nerf gun down and practise your violin" did you not understand?

❖ ❖ ❖

Essential information for parents of young children: Know which of the local playparks dries out the quickest after rain.

❖ ❖ ❖

The 8yr old thinks "pasta" is a swear word. He says he heard it at the local football match.

Slightly unnerving to see a colleague from work in the swimming pool showers. Also brings parenting techniques into sharper focus.

"Mum, see if Killie get into Europe and the Champions League and are in the same group as Manchester United, can we go to the match?" Gotta admire optimism in the 11year olds.

That moment when you have pressed "Send" too soon on the text to the cricket coach. He's a good guy but was probably a bit startled to get a kiss at the end of my text. Oops.

From the 9yr old:

"I'm not gonna lie Mum, there's a girl at swimming that pure fancies me."

"Mum, do you think Sir Alex Ferguson would maybe end his career by coming to be manager of Kilmarnock?"

Ah, the optimism of youth.

The 5yr old tells me that I am not a good enough footballer to attend the 20 mins Mini-Kickers parents' session at the nursery as I'll have to "make goals."

He proceeded to name every man he knew, including the infirm, in the hope that one of them could take my place. After lengthy discussion he conceded I could go, on the condition that the 9yr old gave me some training beforehand.

CHAPTER TWENTY-FIVE: CHRISTMAS

"Christmas comes but once a year!"

And for that, this particular mother is very grateful. There is so much of Christmas that is, or should be, magical with young children. However, for much of the month of December, and the preceding months starting with the time Tesco sneaks in the extra aisle of selection boxes and jumbo tubs of Quality Street, it feels like a prolonged endurance test.

Over and above the usual domestic rigmarole of lunch money, homework and craft projects there are presents to buy, a tree to put up, special meals to prepare, cards to write and a whole host of other commitments that I am coming out in a rash even thinking about.

The school, the nursery and every out-of-school activity has its own Christmas timetable with extra commitments of panto trips, Nativity plays, and Christmas concerts. If I look randomly at the calendar for any day in December and there aren't at least three separate commitments per day written down for each child, I fear I have forgotten something. It doesn't help that one of them also has a birthday in December.

Here are the snippets of life in December – or rather of the Christmas season – which seems to start well before December.

September 1st.
Saturday night and the 4yr old has just staggered past carrying a large red beanbag over his shoulder announcing in the deepest voice he can muster: "Merry Christmas everybody!" And no-one bats an eyelid. We can't even put it down to the full moon - it's just the sort of random event that makes up a typical evening in our house.

September 8th.
The race is on: to finish eating last year's Christmas cake.

October 9th.
The scene: a kitchen in Ayrshire. Husband and wife preparing Sunday lunch. Out of nowhere, one of them starts carefreely humming the first line of a Christmas carol. Editorial constraints prevent me from reporting any more of the conversation between them.

October 14th.
Unexpected 20 min lunch slot without children between morning and afternoon courts. The perfect time to start Christmas shopping.

December 1st.
Fasten your seat belts folks, here comes December!

To the makers of calendars: you're gonna have to make the spaces for December bigger.

A LOT bigger.

December 2nd.
Was greeted this morning with the words:

"Just to say Mum, I've done my Number 2."

He meant advent calendar.

Conversation with the 2yr old: "I'm sorry, but there aren't any builders, monsters, Buzz Lightyears or cats in the Nativity story. You're gonna be a sheep, ok?"

Top tip for Xmas:
Hide the clutter that should have been sorted out in November in the empty boot of the car. The relatives will think you are on top of the housework!

Sorted!

Nativity snippet from middle son: "The bit I liked the best is when he gets smacked with the slipper...."

The mind boggles.

Christmas isn't Christmas until I have recoiled in horror at the price of the Radio Times.

Michael Buble on the car stereo. Two kazoos accompanying him from the back seat. It shouldn't work, but it kinda does.

"I know what I can add to my Christmas list, Mum" says the 4 yr old, "a servant. That's what I'd like for Christmas."

Words fail, and not for the first time.

To all the mums of young children who are doing the Elf Antics for Advent, hats off to you. Meanwhile I will be the parent whose children are in therapy in years to come saying:

"And another thing - my mother never did the elf thing at Christmas...."

Hoping that the spray snow bought on a whim the other week will be just the thing for covering up the dirty fingerprints on the windows.

Asking the 5 yr old what he would like for Christmas.

"Basically just weapons Mum."

Sigh.

Playing the "How Long Will This Diesel Last" game to maximise the savings of the 4p off voucher.

As if December didn't have enough stress already.

Overheard, misheard unseasonal lyrics:

"Last Christmas I gave you my car,
But the very next day you gave it away"

George Michael meets Arnold Clark.

The non-speaking shepherd (6) is thinking about tomorrow's nativity play and musing that really the shepherds should have sticks as it would help keep the sheep in order. I'm hoping the fact that his younger brother is supposed to be a sheep has nothing to do with this...

Christmas get-together at work with the big boss. 20-30 present, coffee and mince pies. All going smoothly until *someone* casually leans on the light switch plunging the (windowless) room into total darkness.

In my defence, switching off saves lighting bills.
#everylittlehelps

December 24th.
The kitchen table is laden with the biggest supermarket shopping of the year. I am trying to pack it away whilst making lunch and simultaneously directing Oldest Son to clean away the myriad of tiny Playmobil pieces from the living room carpet.

The 4yr old seems to think this is an ideal time to share what's on his mind:

"Mum, one day can we get a pet?
A monkey would be good.
Or maybe a turtle?"

Realising I haven't given my usual time warning to the boys to only get up after 8am as of course Ayrshire is Santa's last stop on the mainland before he heads to Ireland.

It could be an early start tomorrow.....

[5am.]

Shun the expensive tech presents - the biggest squeal of delight went to the small bottle of J20 in the stocking.

The most bizarre question of today, heard at 9am this morning:

- What day is it today Mum?
- Christmas Day.
- Oh yes, I forgot.

And the cry went up from the household: "Nice one Santa!" Happy Christmas everyone!

Favourite moments of day: children piling into the bed to ask if Santa has been; catching up with family; the moment before starting to eat Christmas dinner. And a game of table tennis before breakfast.

These hectic Santa years are coming to an end I think, precious times.

You know you're an adult at Christmas when you become fixated on the bin collection days.

I'm going to give him the benefit of the doubt; I think we are out of "t"s.

And so this is Christmas.....

Eating too much chocolate.

Arguments over board games.
Arguments.
Losing the plot over some trivial detail that didn't go right.

It must be time to go back to work.

◆◆◆

ACKNOWLEDGE-
MENTS

I always suspected that I would have to stop recording these stories when the boys became older and more self-conscious. In fact what has happened is that as they grew older each of them could tell their own anecdotes much more wittily than I could. It is therefore time for me to step aside and let them tell their own tales.

To Sons #1, #2 and #3, thank you for all the joy you have brought us over the years and the excellent material for this book.

To my long-suffering husband, thank you for all your support. I may have been the one scribbling down the anecdotes, but the parenting has been done very much together.

EM

Printed in Great Britain
by Amazon

32906368R00069